21 Day Job Search Survival Guide: Maintaining your Peace while Finding your Keep

Carlos Williams

Table of Contents

Preface

My goal for this project is to create a blueprint on how to conduct a productive job search. I believe that a productive job search will create successful outcomes for you on your journey. I'm not sure if people realize that there is an art and a strategy for the job search. With my experience, I know this book would benefit many individuals looking to obtain gainful employment. This book gives step by step instructions on how you, the job seeker, can make effective use of your time during the job search. Included are effective strategies that not only prepare you for an eventful job search but for maintaining your peace during the process. The idea for this book came to me 2 years ago when I decided to go public with my business. I believed that my clients needed something tangible to support them while performing their job search. What I know is that searching for a job can be like a full-time job, and often times, people get discouraged after the first "no" from an employer. This book will show you how to leverage networks, strategize your job search and create an effective plan for success while minimizing feelings of being stress and overwhelmed.

Intro

When it comes to the job search, the job seeker will often jump face forward into the nearest online job board to find a job. Most job seekers will dive in with no plan or sense of direction, just the urge that "I need a job." Some even begin the job search process like a scavenger hunt; if I throw my resume out there, something is bound to happen. The job seeker will log on to one of the job boards such as Indeed.com, Monster.com or even craigslist and search and apply for jobs that they see. Let's not forget in the age of social media, the job seeker has begun to turn to social media outlets such as Facebook and LinkedIn to inquire about job postings. To those who are looking for employment using social media outlets, you must do a little more than simply posting a status that asks your network of friends, "who's hiring?" There is a strategy for crafting a post to inform the reader that you are looking for employment that appeals and compels the reader to send job listings your way.

Leverage all of your resources. Do not limit how you go about obtaining employment. Although online domains have become popular, do not forget to ask friends or family members about employment listings. This is what I like to call "Networking 101." By practicing the art of networking, individuals are not only establishing connections and supports but are able to leverage those connections to reach their goals. If you hone this skill during the job search, it could benefit you in your role once you have gained a new position. Networking in your new position may lead to opportunities to move up in your career and within the company or organization in which you become employed. When leveraging your resources, please be sure to check out the local newspaper for different employment listings. Although these traditional methods may not provide all that you need to apply to an employment opportunity, it gives you a place to start.

Before you begin the job search for the career or employment opportunity that interests you, recognize and understand your worth. If you undervalue yourself or settle for "what you can get," the employer may also undervalue you. Reassure yourself of who you are and what you have to offer. Knowing these things will support you, not only during the job search process but the interviewing process as well. Never give up on your passion because the road isn't clear; instead, clear some of the smoke by staying the course and never giving up. Remember this golden rule—never aspire to be less than what you are. Know your worth.

So, let's take a deep breath and get started!

Week 1
The Journey Begins!

Day 1 & 2
The Job Search

To begin the job search, I believe that the job seeker should start with setting a goal for the number of jobs they plan to apply to for the week. I do recommend that you begin with a manageable number, say 5. Starting the job search to apply to at least 5 job listings helps you with keeping track of the number of applications you have submitted for the week. Also, by setting a goal of a small number of job listings to apply to, it allows the job seeker to compare and contrast the different organizations and how their skills and experiences relate to those particular job listings. Furthermore, it allows the job seeker the opportunity to rank the job listings in order of jobs for which they are well-qualified for or which job listing would be their dream position, but do not necessarily meet all the qualifications.

Once you have your goal set for the week, you should begin using various domains to find those 5 employment opportunities that align with your interest, background and experiences.
Remember, 5 job listings is the most I recommend that you set as a goal. However, if you are satisfied with finding only 3 job listings, that is fine as well.

Create a list of contacts and deadlines for applications.

When it comes to crafting a list of contacts and deadlines for applications, I recommend that you create an Excel file. In your Excel file, you should write down when the application is due and when the review of the application will begin. Doing this not only gives you an idea for when you should have your application submitted but will also give you an idea for when to follow up on the status of your application. Nothing frustrates a recruiter/human resource representative more than receiving too many inquiries on the status of an application by an applicant. Hence, you want to be strategic with how and when you are contacting a recruiter/human resource representative. Do not begin contacting before the application review process. Give the recruiter a week after the application review process begins before reaching out to them. If there is not an application review date, follow up with the employer two weeks after the submission of your application.

Review job requirements, qualifications and preferences

Before you begin your review of the requirements, qualifications and preferences for the position, it is a good practice that you copy and paste these items to a separate word document. This is helpful in the event you need to work offline, or you're unable to find these specifications once an account has been made on the employer's job site. There are times when the applicant portal may not have an overview of job duties. Thus, it is a good idea to have this information to reference, especially when revising your cover letter.

When reviewing the job requirements, qualifications and preferences, you want to look for what element of the position aligns with your skills and experiences. Knowing these factors will support you when creating your cover letter to apply to the position. You will be able to focus on the strengths and experiences that relate to the position that you are applying to. You want to always highlight how your experiences align with the job requirements, qualifications and preferences for the position you are applying to.

Day 3 & 4
Collect your application materials
On days 3 and 4, you should make it your goal to revise your cover letter, update your resume and compile a list of credible references. Having all of these materials readily available provides ease for the job seeker when it comes to uploading application materials.

Revise cover letter to fit the position you are interested in applying to.

There is not a one-size-fits-all method for crafting a cover letter. Still, with strategic formatting, you can pretty much use the same cover letter for each position you are applying for. You have to be sure to revise the cover letter to speak to the position that you are applying to. This may include adding different examples of how your past experiences correlate to the requirements for the position as well as detailing skills that you possess that the employment opportunity may seek in an applicant. If you do not have a cover letter and are not sure how to craft a cover letter, there are a number of online platforms that provide an outline of what a cover letter should include. Some online platforms offer sample cover letters that could be used as a guide to craft your own cover letter.

Update your resume to ensure that it reflects your experience as well as the job requirements being asked.
Like your cover letter, there is not a one-size-fits-all method for crafting your resume. However, once again, if you are strategic when crafting your resume, you can use it to apply to a wide variety of jobs. I recommend that all people have both a chronological resume and a functional resume on hand to support them during the job application process. Knowing which type of resume to use when applying to jobs is what you will need to be clear on before submitting your

application. Overall, a chronological resume is used to list past job experiences. A functional resume, on the other hand, is often used when an individual lacks direct work experience but have learned experiences (skills) that relate to the positions they hope to obtain. Whichever resume you decide to use, you want to ensure that it speaks to the job you are applying to. Also, the employer can clearly understand that you are capable of completing the task required for the position.

Compile a list of Credible References

Always remember to create a list of 5 to 6 personal/professional references that will speak to your skills, ability, and experience. Please be sure to speak with these references to ensure they will give you a good recommendation or be a credible reference for you. Also, forward a copy of your resume to the individual you choose to be your reference. This will allow the individual to have a full understanding of all of your experiences and skills so they can speak directly to your ability to be successful on the job. These references will be rotated based on the top reference the employer is asking for. Be sure to have a mixture of professional and character-based references. Most employers will either ask from one or both types of references, so it's good that you have a good number of both.

Day 5 & 6
Application Submissions
For days 5 and 6, you should be ready to submit any applications for jobs you are interested in.

Apply to job postings. Submitting any assessments and uploading all documents.
Have all of your supporting documents available to apply to the position you are interested in obtaining. This is inclusive of your resume, cover letter, references, reference letters, and sometimes, your high school/college transcripts.

Also, allow enough time in the day to complete assessments that come with the application. Most assessments take anywhere between 30 to 45 minutes to complete. So, you want to ensure that your computer/laptop is fully charged, and you are in a quiet space. Also, ensure your internet connection is efficient, and you have set aside time to complete the application thoroughly.

Keep a record of when you applied for each position.
Keep an excel document of the date you applied to a position and the contact person/hiring manager. Create a two-week window to follow up with the contact person, hiring manager, recruiter or Human Resource Representative. Remember to not begin contacting the recruiter/human resources representative before the application review process. Give a week

following the commencement of the application review process before reaching out to them. If there is not an application review date, follow up with the employer two weeks after the submission of your application.

Day 7
It's time to take a break! Treat yourself! Break Time!
Do something fun, something relaxing! Self-care is crucial when you are performing a job search. At times, doing a productive job search can seem like a full-time job, so it's important that you make time to decompress and rejuvenate from the work you accomplished during the week. It's okay to reward yourself, even if you feel that you haven't accomplished much. You are doing great work, and you don't want to tire yourself out too soon. This is the beginning of creating a work/life balance, and this practice could carry over to your lifestyle once employment is reached.

On the next page, I have provided space for you to determine goals you would like to set for your first week on the job search. Feel free to use this page to write notes, keep track of task and prepare for the following week. You got this!

Week 1 Goals:

_____

_____

_____

_____

_____

_____

_____

_____

_____

_____

Week 2
Staying the Course!

Stay the course and repeat!
Around week two, you may begin to feel a little anxious. For some reason, we often feel that if we've applied for a job, we should get a call back the next day to request an interview, forgetting that with anything in life, there is a process. Being invited for an interview comes with a process. Also, reviewing applications comes with a process for the reviewer. Several factors affect the delay in contact for an interview request. The application may be reviewed by a committee, and that committee may have difficulty with finding times that everyone on the committee is available to review applications and send requests for interviews. Also, life happens, and application reviewers may be out sick, have a family emergency or even be on vacation.

So, it is important that you exercise patience and understanding during this time. Don't forget to set goals for the week, and don't lose sight of those goals.

Day 8 & 9
Read the local newspaper and job boards
Use Day 8 and 9 to look through the local newspaper and job boards to see if any career fairs are happening during the week or in the

coming weeks. Figure out the date, time and location of the career fairs/job fairs and see if you can attend multiple in a day. Another place that many individuals do not think to check for career fairs is with the institutions from which they graduated. Although career fairs at various institutions (universities, community colleges, high schools and etc.) are geared towards current students, most employers wouldn't mind someone who has already obtained (or about to obtain) the degree needed to fulfill the various positions for which they are advertising.

Day 10 & 11
Job Search
Once again, use various search engines to find 5 employment opportunities that align with your interest, background or experiences. Remember that 5 is the maximum, and it is perfectly fine if you can only find 2 to 3 job listings that you are interested in applying to. Once you have read through the listing and decided that you would like to apply to these positions, add these new employment opportunities and deadlines for applications to the list compiled from the previous week. Remember that you've done this before, so this is nothing new. Regain your focus, your composure and let's get to it.

Day 12 & 13
Apply to jobs, submitting any assessments and uploading all documents.

Once again, you would want to have all of your supporting documents available for applying for the position you are interested in obtaining. This is inclusive of your resume, cover letter, references, reference letters, and sometimes, your college transcripts.

Also, allow enough time in the day to complete the assessments that come with the application. Most assessments take anywhere between 30 to 45 minutes to complete. So, ensure that your computer/laptop is fully charged and that you are in a quiet space. Also, check that your internet connection is efficient, and you have set aside time to complete the application fully. Be intentional about minimizing distractions when you are completing assessments. You do not want to allow the smallest infraction of failing an assessment to keep you from obtaining that position for which you are completing the assessment.

Keep a record of when you applied for each position.

Be sure to add these new positions to your ongoing Excel document. Include the date you applied to the position and the contact person/hiring manager. Allow a two-week window to follow up with the contact person, hiring manager, recruiter or Human Resource Representative. Remember to not begin contacting the recruiter/human resources representative before the application review process. Give a week after the application review process begins before reaching out to them. If there is not an application review date, follow up with the employer two weeks after the submission of your application.

Day 14
Take a Break!

We've approached that moment in the week, where it's time to take a break. You've worked hard all week, so find something relaxing to do and enjoy yourself. Life is full of stressors, and job searching can be stressful, so find a moment to do something you enjoy or find something that brings you peace and comfort. Whether it's going to a religious service, a pick-up game with your friends or a nice hike/walk. Do what is needed to decompress and make yourself whole.

On the next page, I have provided space for you to determine goals you would like to set for your second week on the job search. Feel free to use this page to write notes, keep track of task and prepare for the following week. You got this!

Week 2 Goals:

_____

_____

_____

_____

_____

_____

_____

_____

_____

_____

_____

_____

Week 3
Working through Redundancy!

You have reached week 3, and at this point, redundancy with the job search may become overwhelming. During this week, it is time to become unorthodox in our approach to finding gainful employment. By this time, you are probably tired of sitting in front of your computer screen, searching for different employment opportunities. This would be an excellent time to get dressed and get moving.

Day 15 & 16
Go on/Request Informational Interview!
Grab your best professional outfit, print out at least 10 copies of your resume and go on what I like to call "informational interviews." Informational interviews are designed for you to go in and ask questions of the employer regarding possible opportunities to work with the current employer. During this time, you should ask the employer their current needs, the culture of the organization and see what areas the employer is looking to grow. From there, you should be able to assess and communicate how your skills and experiences fit the needs of the organization.

By dropping in on employers or requesting informational interviews, you show initiative and a willingness to work, regardless of being offered a job. In the technology age, we are used to completing everything online, that we miss out on that human connection. Remember, although a system may check your application to ensure that it meets the minimum requirements, a human will be offering you the job. So, put on your best threads, say a prayer and take a walk of courage to create an opportunity for success. Remember that you are a walking marketing tool, so be sure to practice your "30-second elevator pitch" and proceed with patience and confidence.

Note: If you do not have a professional outfit and are low on funds, it is okay to visit your local Goodwill or Thrift shop to find professional wear. Also, ask family members if they have items you can wear.

Day 17 & 18
Coffee Date/Lunch Date!
Use this time to go on a lunch date with a mentor or a friend to pick their brain for updates on the job market. Ask them questions on whether they've heard of any job fairs or employment opportunities. Practice interview skills, print out mock interview questions and have this individual ask you questions that would possibly be asked during an interview. Practice your 15-second elevator pitch in front of them and ask them how you can improve your technique. Also, this would be a good time to ask these

individuals about your strengths and weaknesses. Asking this individual about your strengths and weaknesses gives insight into what you are doing right and how you can grow. Nine times out of 10, you will be asked about your strengths and weaknesses during an interview. It's good to know this, so you can begin to craft your responses when asked about it.

Day 19 & 20
Check In on your Application Status!

On a job posting, some employers may state not to contact them; however, for the employers that don't, it is okay to reach out to them to inquire about the application status and review of your application. You can either do this with a phone call or via email. With this communication, be sure to include your name, the position you applied for and reiterate why you are the optimal candidate for the position. It is a good practice to rehearse what you have to say before contacting the employer.

Follow up on the positions you previously applied to in the previous two weeks. Craft a generic email inquiring about the status of your application. Emailing is the best option for contacting an employer. Most employers will state on their job posting that phone calls are not accepted. If the employer does not place restrictions for contacting and if you are eager, feel free to contact the employer by phone. Once again, when contacting the employer, it is a good idea to rehearse what you would like to say and ask good follow up questions.

Day 21
Take a Break, Re-group and Re-energize!

Once again, it's time to treat yourself for the hard work you've put in throughout the week. Make a habit of rewarding yourself at the end of the workweek. It gives you something to look forward to and minimizes the feeling of defeat in the event that you do not hear back from an employer within the week. Your reward to yourself does not have to cost money; it could simply be a trip to a bookstore, movie night with a friend or a phone call with your favorite relative. Whatever you do, take a break, re-group and gain your energy.

On the next page, I have provided space for you to determine goals you would like to set for your third week on the job search. Feel free to use this page to write notes, keep track of task and prepare for the following week. You got this!

Week 3 Goals:

_____

_____

_____

_____

_____

_____

_____

_____

_____

_____

_____

Conclusion
Never lose sight of your Goals!

The goal is to be creative, trying not to be too repetitive with your methods and mechanism. Your goal is to find fresh ways to execute your job search and task. For some, searching for a job may be a daunting task, but it doesn't have to be. With an effective strategy, you will find and obtain gainful employment before you know it. Never lose sight of the fact that unemployment is temporary and know your dream job/career is in your view.

One thing that I forgot to mention earlier when applying for jobs on various domains is that you want to ensure that you are applying directly to the job site. For instance, if you find a job listing on craigslist, please do not simply reply to the craigslist post. I recommend that you create a separate email and email the contact at the end of the job posting. Another good practice is to apply directly to the job listing on the employer's website. There are several phishing scams, so it is important to be careful to protect yourself and your information.

In all, whether you are on the job search or currently employed, remember to keep an updated list of references and your resume current. You never know when an opportunity to move into the career of your dreams will present itself. Remember to never give up on your goals and dreams. Your next "yes" is just around the corner!

Notes:

_____

_____

_____

_____

_____

_____

_____

_____

_____

_____

_____

_____

_____

Appendix

Sample Email Follow Up for Application

Good Afternoon **[Insert Name or Human Resources Manager]**

My name is **[Insert Name]**, and I am writing to follow up on the application I submitted for the **[Position Title]** with **[Company's Name]** on **[Insert Date Application was submitted]**. I believe I am an optimal candidate for this position as I possess […**here you want to list skills and experiences that relate to the position you applied for]**. I would love to discuss how my skills and experiences are relevant to this position and how I can be an asset to your company. Please feel free to contact me if you have any questions or concerns.
I look forward to hearing from you soon.

Thank you for your time and consideration

[Your Name]

Questions to Help Prepare for the Interview

1. Tell me about yourself?
2. Name your strengths?
3. Name your weaknesses?
4. What role do you play in a team?
   a. Sharper, Implementer, Completer/Finisher, Coordinator, Team Worker, Resource Investigator, Monitor-Evaluator, Specialist, Plants
5. Why do you want this job?
6. How well do you work in a team?
7. Name a time you've experienced conflict with a coworker/teammate. How did you resolve the conflict?
8. How do you deal with conflict on the job?
9. Name a time you went beyond the call of duty on the job?
10. Why do you want to work for this company?
11. Why do you want this job?
12. Why should we hire you?

Informational Interview

How to request an Informational Interview

You can request Informational Interviews through Mentorship or Research. Simply email or call the Administrative Assistant, CEO, Manager or etc., of the establishment and ask if you could meet with them to discuss the organization, their roles and/or how they came into the business. People love talking about themselves, so match your approach and be genuine and sincere.

Goals for Informational Interviews
- Gain a better understanding of the workplace environment.
- Gain a better understanding of how you can support the organization/business.
- Gain a better understanding of how your experiences and skills fit in a current role in the organization or how you can create a role to support the organization.
- Gain a better understanding of the needs of the organization.

Sample Email Follow Up After Interview

Good Afternoon [**Interviewer**],

My name is [**Insert Name**], and I recently interviewed for the [**Insert Position Title**] position. I really enjoyed meeting everyone and having the opportunity to meet with the staff at [**Insert Company's Name**]. I am writing to follow up on the interview and hiring process. I believe that I am an optimal candidate for this position because I am dedicated and possess exceptional organizational, communication and interpersonal skills. I believe if given the opportunity, I would be able to support the company with increasing productivity while maintaining a culture of quality and professionalism.
I look forward to hearing from someone soon about the status of this position. If you have any questions or concerns, please do not hesitate to contact me by phone or email at [**XXX-XXX-XXXX**] or john.doe16@gmail.com

Thank you for your time and consideration,

John Doe

About the Arthur

Carlos Williams is the founder of Career Pitch, LLC., a premier Career Consulting Firm that specializes in career development by training individuals on how to effectively communicate their experiences. Carlos earned his Master's in Educational Psychology and has over 8 years of experience with providing guidance and instruction to individuals who are looking to obtain the career of their dreams. Furthermore, Career Pitch, LLC., offers resume and cover letter development and interviewing techniques and preparation. For individuals who have experienced stumbling blocks in life, we provide support in creating letters of explanation that effectively explain a criminal history.

Visit Us Today: www.career-pitch.com
Email: info@career-pitch.com

www.ingramcontent.com/pod-product-compliance
Lightning Source LLC
Chambersburg PA
CBHW061654050426
42443CB00027B/3295